"Living a life of abundance, wealth, peace, and continued expansion requires a strong spiritual connection. Denise Stillman shows us how to see clearly the four essential levers we need to pull to live the bountiful life we are all meant to live. A powerful teaching!"

—Karen Russo, MBA, award-winning author of *The Money Keys* and sought-after spiritual wealth-building expert

"Clarity is key when it comes to getting what you want in life. Living intentionally, planning for what you desire versus hoping someone will hand it to you, is the foundation of all success. Denise's book awakens your spirit to find that at the core of your being is all you need to realize the power you already possess to build the life of your dreams. All you need to do is unleash it!"

—Ret. Lt. Col. Dan Roose, business consultant and founder of No Greater Wealth, and contributor to *Visionaries With Guts!*

"Denise's book helps you unearth your values and shows you how to weave them throughout your daily life to breathe more meaning into all you do. By taking massive action in all areas—your family life and your relationship with money and your business—you can reach goals you never thought possible. The most important thing is to stop making excuses for why you're not happy. You *are* the solution. Now, ready, go!"

—Loral Langemeier, CEO and founder of Live Out Loud (www.liveoutloud.com)**, and best-selling author of the three-book Millionaire Maker series and *Put More Cash in Your Pocket***

COURAGEOUS CLARITY

FOUR KEYS TO UNLOCK THE LEADER INSIDE

DENISE STILLMAN, MBA

iUniverse, Inc.
Bloomington

Courageous Clarity
Four Keys to Unlock the Leader Inside

Special pricing on bulk purchases of *Courageous Clarity: Four Keys to Unlock the Leader Inside* is available.

For more information, visit www.courageousclaritythebook.com.

iUniverse books may be ordered through booksellers or by contacting:

iUniverse
1663 Liberty Drive
Bloomington, IN 47403
www.iuniverse.com
1-800-Authors (1-800-288-4677)

ISBN: 978-1-4620-2776-7 (sc)
ISBN: 978-1-4620-2777-4 (e)

Printed in the United States of America

iUniverse rev. date: 08/08/2011

DEDICATION

To my mother, whose belief in me and creativity constantly inspired. To my father, whose shared work ethic keeps me going. To my sisters, who always keep me guessing. To my brothers, watching over me from above. And to God, my mentors, Mike, Claire, and John, who help me focus on what's really important in life.

"Commit to the Lord whatever you do, and your plans will succeed." Proverbs 16:3

"Knowing others is wisdom; knowing the self is enlightenment. Mastering others requires force; mastering the self needs strength."

—Lao Tzu, Chinese philosopher

CONTENTS

FOREWORD

Many of us live our lives on the sidelines. By that, I mean, we do not fully jump into the game of life, learn ways to best play the game and really take action to improve our performance with and satisfaction from the game. Life is meant to be fun and to be lived abundantly, happily, richly and deeply. Our ultimate purpose in the game of life is to create and grow relationships with others, one human touch at a time. *Courageous Clarity: Four Keys to Unlock the Leader Inside* is a terrific guide to more fully develop your life's playbook.

There is nothing more important than growing relationships through being present in the moment and getting to know others to learn how you may be able to help them. One of the ways I grow each day is by networking everywhere and anywhere I can. However, I don't network to find out what someone can do for me. I network to find out how I can "reach out and touch someone" by helping them. In fact, I've developed a 5/10/15 contact system for networking that I explain in my latest <u>New York Times</u> best-selling book *Networking is a Contact Sport*. Forget growing your number of "friends" on your Facebook account just for the sake of having a higher number of contacts. The human touch always trumps technology and you truly grow as a person only when you meet someone face-to-face, look them in the eye and send positivity into the universe by helping them.

Both Denise Stillman and I are entrepreneurs who believe in the indomitable power of the human spirit and the unlimited possibilities available to all of us. This book not only gives you a very simple, yet powerful, way to examine your behaviors that may be limiting your progression toward your goals – it also describes in detail specific ways to remove what is blocking your growth toward success in many areas of your life: your business, your relationships, your spirituality and more.

One of the best ways you can begin to move toward your goals and dreams is to change your mindset and move toward positivity in every area of your life, especially if you are starting a new chapter, whether it be through a job or career change or building a new business. Utilizing the tools Denise provides in *Courageous Clarity* and online at www.courageousclaritythebook.com, you will begin to clear your mind, your heart and your spirit of what may be preventing you from living your "wish I had" life and reaching the heights of success both Denise and I know are possible.

My advice to you is to read *Courageous Clarity* and use the fourth key – action – to unlock your leader inside. Your path to unbridled success will be much more evident and you will be on your way to a life you've only dreamed of until this point. And, who knows? Maybe you'll find inspiration to begin building your own successful business, too.

Joe Sweeney
Speaker on Networking Success and
Author of *Networking is a Contact Sport*
NY Times best seller, #2 *Wall Street Journal*
and #1 *USA Today* best seller

ACKNOWLEDGMENTS

I've had this book in my head and heart for more than a decade. However, I was able to write it only after I "came up for air" from a hamster-wheel kind of life when I voluntarily hopped off the employed freight train and onto the entrepreneur express.

What inspired me greatly to write this book is the phrase "I don't know how you do it," which I heard at least one hundred times in my nearly 20-year career in marketing, strategy, and business development thus far, particularly during the latter 11 years of it while my husband and I began raising our family. People kept asking, so I thought I owed them an answer. Well, here it is. This is how I did it—and continue to do so.

Unlike other self-help books that offer abstract concepts to consider, *Courageous Clarity* gives you a concrete system for reviewing your life activity and tested strategies to change that behavior to move you in the direction you choose.

I'd like to acknowledge the following people who helped me polish this work and make it clearer for you: Dan Roose, Denise Bach, Sandy Couch, Shannon Schroeder, Abby Shelton, Bob Stillman, Nicolle Heller, Debi Vera, Amy Sanders, Shelton Matsey, Sarah Victory and Dr. Dan. Thank you for being friends and supportive guides along this journey called life. Blessings to all of you!

CHAPTER 1

8━┓

DISCOVERING YOUR EMPTY PLACE

If you have a job in today's economy, you can be thankful; you will appreciate what you have even more by reading this book. If you don't have a job, you *really* need to read this book as you journey into your next venture. Many workers are going to their jobs out of necessity to put food on the table, but they are miserable where they are. In fact, 26,000 workers have shared several common reasons why they are unhappy. The most stressed of the workers surveyed said that too much work, their bosses' behavior, and long hours were the top causes of discontent.[1]

I'm not sure the respondents carefully considered their answers about their sources of unhappiness. I'd like to challenge the notion that work-related issues are the true source of most stress. Collectively, many of my mentors, including my primary one from "up above," proclaim that happiness comes from within. I used to believe that was just a good story until my personal journey in the last several years revealed this truth to my core being.

You see, at my last job, I worked with a woman who nearly always had a complaint on her lips. However, when I asked Cathy Roman[2] why she seemed so unhappy every time I passed her desk, she spoke of the same problems each time I saw her, and most of them were outside of work. She was a beautiful woman with a sparkling smile and a great laugh that I, unfortunately, didn't get to hear very often. From her stories, it seemed life had dealt her some bad cards: an early divorce that forced her to raise her son alone, health issues that made it difficult for her to exercise, her son's unemployment, and so on. She had negative comments about her neighbors, her home repairs, her church, her physician, and many other facets of her overall very good life. But very few were about her work situation. I always tried to take Cathy to the brighter side of her conversation but, regrettably, never had enough time to share with her what I am about to share with you.

I've often wondered why many of us are still not satisfied at the end of a full day of activity, whether it's a workday or not. Do you ever stop to think about why your life is not more fulfilling? Whether you are employed/unemployed/underemployed, a business owner, or an unpaid caregiver for children or other family members, underlying our daily routines is a strong current of positive, life-giving, happy energy that many do not even know exists. As infants and young children, we certainly knew that source, but years of education, life experiences, and exposure to negative influences in our society have buried that energy source. Until you unearth that energy and then find ways to focus it toward what you really want in life, you may never know the abundance you were meant to receive. I only recently took this very personal journey and unleashed an explosion of energy in my life. I want to help you do the same.

"Everybody Gets a Car," According to Oprah

You see, I was one of the 276 winners of a Pontiac G6 as a guest in the audience for the 19th season premiere of the "Oprah Show" in September 2004. About 30 minutes into the taping of the show, Oprah's staff handed each audience member a small silver and white box. Just before she allowed us to open our boxes, Oprah told us that if our box contains a key, we will win a car. I vividly recall the moment I opened my silver and white box to find a shiny "Oprah Show" key ring tied to a red ribbon with a car key on it. I jumped up and down and screamed and soon realized *all* of us, including my sister next to me, were jumping up and down screaming, holding the same key ring, red ribbon and car key. Then, Oprah proclaimed, "You get a car! Everybody gets a car!" After we hugged all of our neighbors and the squeals of excitement from the audience ceased, we were instructed to walk outside to the back lot where we were released to choose our car. I recall the moment I came face-to-face with Oprah, exhuberantly thanked her, then explained to her that I needed to run quickly to pick out the car I wanted to take home. After that, I ducked under her right arm that was outstretched to the G6 next to which she stood and raced to my new car.

It is no accident that my sister and I were invited to attend that episode of "Oprah." I know I attracted that very unique and fun diversion in my life by the good I was seeking to do for my sister who needed help at the time. I firmly believe that we each have the power to create what it is we desire in our lives. We just need to know how, and I know that I have discovered a way to source the energy to create positive experiences in my life.

Many do not know this source of energy exists because either they are not in tune with what truly fulfills them in life or the energy current is buried under layers of unsuccessful attempts to find satisfaction. To get to that strong current of energy, we need to clear the clutter within and discover what I call our *"empty place."* Believe it or not, that empty place really isn't empty at all. We'll discuss more about this contradiction in future chapters. Your empty place, filled with your life's unique recipe for abundance, is actually like the water source of a natural spring that continually brings to the surface a flow of powerful, life-giving energy you can use to fuel your business, your relationships, your physical well-being—all aspects of your life.

Spiritual leaders often speak of the "God-shaped" empty place inside all of us that only spirituality can fulfill. Now, I know deeply that my faith has certainly shaped my life and filled the strong foundation of my empty place. However, I believe the contents of our empty places are intertwined with many other influences in our lives. I know that you first must find your empty place to find clues about who you are. The earlier in life you discover who you truly are, the more opportunity you'll have to harness this strong current of energy and enrich your life by clearly leading it — through rewarding relationships, business success, spiritual connection with a higher power, vitality, financial prosperity, and more.

We Are Not What the World Tells Us

You see, we are not defined by the titles we have at work, at home, and in our families. Amy Beers in Pennsylvania, who was profiled on USAToday.com[3], went from vice president of sales to bartender during the 2009 recession. She said, at first, she felt ashamed because she no longer carried that big title. She now realizes that she values the health she and her son share and is patiently waiting for what life will offer her next.

We are not the sum of what the world tells us. We are defined by what *we tell the world*. We communicate who we are by how we fill the empty place we all have inside of us. Our choice of "filler" for our empty place is what makes each of us unique. What we choose to fill ourselves with can make us wonderful and powerful individuals—or can weaken our potential.

Notice that I'm talking about selectively choosing what we put inside our empty place. By being aware that we have a conscious choice to make, we begin to realize that we are responsible for the impact our filler has on our lives. Being very clear about what's truly inside your empty place at this point in your life can help you discover the source of much of your spiritual connection with a higher power (or lack thereof). It also helps you understand the reason for your levels of happiness, rewarding relationships, business success, and much more.

Our empty place is really at the core of our living. But how do we find our empty place and what's inside of it? It may sound like a complex scavenger hunt, but it's really not very difficult. However, it does require some introspection. You need to look inside your life and ask yourself the key Courageous Clarity questions:

- What do I do when I first awake?
- What are my first thoughts? Words?
- What motivates me to get out of bed when I want to stay under the covers?
- Who in my life makes me most happy when I'm with them?
- What do I listen to on the radio/my MP3 player/my CD player?
- What kind of music lifts my mood when I listen to it?
- How much TV do I watch each day, and what do I watch?
- What do I say when I talk to myself (you know, when you're looking in the mirror or when you're commenting on something you just did)? We all do it… whether it's actually spoken or is just a thought.
- What am I moving toward? What are my dreams?
- What is my vision for my life?
- Who will care about my contributions to life after I'm gone?
- What do I want people to say (and not say) at my funeral?

Make a list of your responses to these questions. You can download this list to your computer from www.courageousclaritythebook.com /emptyplace to simplify this task. Be sure to save your answers for later reflection. Your answers to these questions reveal a great deal about who you are inside. You can find your empty place by following the trail from what you put into the depths of your soul. Once you discover your empty place, you'll know what's missing in your life. Using the four keys to Courageous Clarity as your guide (we'll talk about them in chapter 2), you'll find new ways to fill your empty place with the right "recipe" for you to unlock your life's full leadership potential.

It wasn't until I discovered the four keys to Courageous Clarity that I was able to be honest with myself about the shape of my empty place and what I was pouring into it. When I learned my *current* recipe for clarity (yes, it will change during each season of your life), I was able to set my life on a path toward a clear vision and unlock an *amazing* source of abundant energy. *I want the same for you* and your business and your relationships—your whole life.

When you are truly honest with yourself, what you find in your empty place may surprise you. Tony Robbins, one of my mentors, says we all move toward pleasure and away from pain. I believe that is true. As human beings, we are programmed to seek pleasure and shun pain. However, I believe what we're really trying to do is to fill our empty place with pleasant experiences. How we seek that pleasure makes all the difference in our ability to unlock our life's leadership potential. Some fill that yearning for pleasure with what I call "power blockers"—such as excessive alcohol, smoking, or drugs, while others turn to too much time at work and other negative behaviors.

Not everyone requires the same elements to successfully fill their empty place. In fact, in many instances, it's not what we take from the world to put into our empty place but what we give to the world that actually creates fulfillment. What the four keys to Courageous Clarity will reveal to you is your own ability to discover what's important in your life, in your business, in your relationships, in everything you do. Then, you will be able to create this amazing abundance of life-giving energy, peace, and the ability to attract all the positivity that this life has to offer you—*and you it*. So, read on and learn the four keys to Courageous Clarity that will help you unlock the leader within you.

CHAPTER 2

WHAT IS COURAGEOUS CLARITY?

Each day, we have so many opportunities to improve our lives and the lives of those around us. Humans are amazingly complex and fascinating creatures. Have you ever just stopped all that you are doing and observed humans in an airport, on the street, or in a shopping mall for 15 minutes? Each of us has unique environmental influences and cellular codes that define who we are, what decisions we make, and how we walk, talk, think, appreciate, love, give, share, compete, become all that we can be, and much more.

Imagine how much more enjoyable this world would be if each of us could truly focus on what's important in our lives and create a sense of harmony, abundance, and fulfillment. Now, I realize that may not be possible 100 percent of the time for 100 percent of the population for many reasons, including geopolitical and socioeconomic factors; however, we need to strive for ideals to attempt to bring them to life. In my journey, many tools and tactics have helped bring me to where I am today. When I evaluate what helped bring me to the mind-set and success I have, I realize the process mirrors what I do for my strategic planning clients, who seek my assistance to bring their companies to more productive, profitable levels.

I can simplify my process for you into four keys to this concept of Courageous Clarity to help you begin filling your empty place with your unique ingredients for the life you want to lead—in business, your personal relationships, your health, and more. The four keys Courageous Clarity are:

- Congruence
- Aspiration
- Intent
- Action

We'll explore what each key means, and in the next chapter, I'll show you how you can create a path for these keys to easily work their way into your life.

Congruence

Do you remember your school lessons in geometry? My geometry teacher, Mr. Kevin McCleary, taught me that two triangles are considered congruent if their corresponding sides are equal in length and their corresponding angles are equal in size. In other words, the shapes *are similar to* and *agree with* one another. For those who have studied psychology or neurolinguistic programming, congruence is the concept of internal and external consistency in your world.

Congruence is the state of being true to your real self as you present yourself to the world and give back to it. One source of true happiness is found in what we bring into the world versus what we take from it. However, we cannot unlock our full ability to give to others if we are not authentic. Some people live by the motto, "What you see is what you get." This has to be completely true if you are to free your potential. It's exhausting to present a persona in public that is in disharmony with the "real you." Not only does this behavior drain your energy; it distracts you from unlocking your true potential.

Now, many will argue with me that many of our work roles dictate that we are someone different at work from who we are at home with our family and friends. And, yes, I agree to an extent. For instance, thousands of high-powered female business executives by day convert to dutiful wives and child caretakers in the evening. The roles are different, but underlying the actions in each of the roles *must* be the same purposes. One such purpose could be integrity. The executive makes each decision in her life at work and home on the basis that it must be steeped in honesty and produce a truthful result. Now, the communication styles the executive uses at work will most likely be very different from those she uses at home, but the reason she does what she does must be similar to her beliefs and her purposes. If she has *agreement* in *why* she does what she does in her career and home life and what she believes at her deepest core, congruence exists and her potential is unleashed. Since women just surpassed men in total numbers in the workplace and women-owned small businesses are projected to be responsible for creating one-third of the 15.3 million new U.S. jobs anticipated by the Bureau of Labor Statistics by 2018,[4] American women executives, in particular, have great potential to create congruence in their lives and serve as an example of Courageous Clarity for their peers, employees and families.

There must be a state of agreement—a coming together—of one's core values in what we pursue in our work lives and personal lives for there to be an energy flow. For you to get closer to this key, you must first define your core values and consciously and daily choose to live by them. If you've never defined your core values, which really never should change in your adult life or in your business, you must do this first to get closer to unlocking your life's leadership power. We'll discuss how to determine your core values in the next chapter.

Before we move on to the next key to Courageous Clarity, I must say a word about relationships and congruence. The concept of congruence plays a huge role in how we relate to one another, particularly a partner or spouse. For us to assess congruence, we must evaluate the respective relationships of one thing to another. Remember the triangles? Congruent triangles *are similar to* and *agree with* one another. In relationships, it may be easier to relate to those with whom we share a level of congruence.

A Google® search reveals more than 4.5 million references for the importance of relationships in life.[5] A popular preacher on American Christian radio, Dr. Michael Youssef, founding pastor of The Church of The Apostles and president of the ministry Leading the Way in Atlanta, says frequently that the primary reason we are here on earth is to form relationships. Dynamic Catholic author Matthew Kelly coined the phrase that my husband and I have on our kitchen wall at home: "We are on this earth to help each other become a better version of ourselves."[6] I wholeheartedly agree with both of them. In life, as in business, most of our happiness and feelings of success usually stem from enjoyable and profitable relationships, right?

> *"There are certain things that are fundamental to human fulfillment. The essence of these needs is captured in the phrase 'to live, to love, to learn, to leave a legacy.' The need to live is our physical need for such things as food, clothing, shelter, economical well-being, health. The need to love is our social need to relate to other people, to belong, to love and to be loved. The need to learn is our mental need to develop and to grow. And the need to leave a legacy is our spiritual need to have a sense of meaning, purpose, personal congruence, and contribution."*
> *– Dr. Stephen R. Covey*

One of ways to unlock the leader inside is to find *from which* relationships you derive the most value and *to which* relationships you can contribute the most value. Ask yourself, "Does how I spend my time (both personally and in my business) reflect a focus on developing meaningful relationships?" As in life, success in business comes from surrounding yourself with people to whom you can contribute—and who can contribute to your pursuits. There is no substitute for having a great team (of friends, family, and business colleagues). There's no such thing as a self-made millionaire, according to Loral Langemeier, one of my mentors and the proclaimed "Millionaire Maker" and money expert.[7] So, you must pursue meaningful relationships as you seek congruence in your life.

Aspiration

The second key to Courageous Clarity is aspiration. When we think about what we really want to aspire to in our lives, our human minds can wander in many directions, and the images are usually somewhat hazy. Some of us might say "more time with our families and less time at work" or "to retire early" or "to read a book on a beautiful beach" or "better health." But those are just vague snapshots of the full dream. To move us from those blurry images of happiness—one of the greatest profits in life—we need to become better, clearer dreamers. We need to feel free to be very bold and specific about our dreams.

> *"When your belief in you and your dream is greater than your belief in other people's opinions, you will have mastered your life."*
> *– Johnna Parr, Author of* **When the Dream is Big Enough**

Our human capacity for dreaming is immense. Many of us just need to get out of our own way and allow ourselves to think about fuller, bigger possibilities and how we can pursue what we really want in life. Why do I say this? Because there exists a higher power that truly wants you to be happy and to live the life you are meant to live. My higher power is God. Others may refer to that power by a different name. But just the same, there is a higher power at work that we need to be in tune with to unlock the leadership of our lives.

Dream Like You Were Seven Again

Can you recall what life felt like as a seven-year-old with your life ahead of you and the ability to dream of becoming whatever you wanted to be? Our son, who is now 10, has wanted to be a Major League Baseball player for years. As a secondary plan, he'll be an attorney, but he's pretty convinced he'll be a baseball player. I think that's terrific. We encourage him to dream about that possibility so much that we are helping him develop what his dream looks like from many aspects to make it more real in his mind. We talk about what team will recruit him, what position he'll play, what his number will be, what he'll be famous for, and so on. We do all we can to help him paint into the corners of that dream so he can almost smell the professional baseball field, hear the fans cheering his name, and see himself performing well in the World Series.

It is with this same boldness, this same clarity that we must dream. We can make our own lives—our entire world—so much better through the visualization of what is possible. As adults, we tend to permit our rational minds to place all the potential barriers we can think of in front of our dreams before they have time to sprout. We let our negative self-talk ("you're too young," "you're too old," "you can't afford it," "you're not smart enough," and so on) squeeze the life out of our dreams before they take root in our minds and hearts. Why do we do this? Some are fearful and some prefer the status quo, while others have lost that childlike view that anything's possible. I would argue that, without this raw imagination, we lose vital energy that is needed to contribute to others and to this world. Without it, we can't add much value to this life and certainly cannot tap into our leadership power. Another favorite quote from Matthew Kelly's book I mentioned earlier is, "Life is about adding value. Contribute or die."

At Casanova's on the Waterfront

It's never too late to create your dreams. I personally have more than 10 statements that create a detailed picture of what I want my life to look like at specific times in the near future. You can be 85 and still dream about the wonderful possibilities you want ahead in your life—such as spending the next holiday on Grand Cayman with your best friend and parasailing with him four hundred feet above the aqua-blue North

Sound on a deliciously warm, sunny day in January, followed by a relaxing, hot stone massage on the beach and a bottle of red wine with a four-course meal on the waterfront at Casanova's, with the sea lapping gently at the beach below. Now, that's the type of specificity we need in our dreams! We need to create definite timeframes, visceral feelings and emotions, and clear perceptions about what we want in our futures. We need to know it so intimately that we can say it today to begin creating the belief that it is real, that we know what the end result will be. Then, we need to choose to live with our compass pointed in that direction, which is the next key to Courageous Clarity.

> *"Go confidently in the direction of your dreams.*
> *Live the life you have imagined."*
> *– Henry David Thoreau, American Essayist,*
> *Poet and Philosopher*

Intent

Another important strategic planning concept is beginning with the end in mind. This doesn't mean you need to calculate each step of your life or business before you make a move toward your dreams. It does mean, however, that you will develop a mental and physical picture of the aspirations you've dreamed for yourself, your loved ones, and the world around you and you will live each day with the purpose of making those aspirations reality. The road map for getting to your desired outcome will be revealed along the way with the proper team surrounding you. The process of developing your intention is most effective when you develop intentions that are in the not-too-distant future, such as three to five years ahead.

Some success theorists refer to this as your "why," the reason you want to reach for a dream. It also can be referred to as living intentionally rather than allowing life to simply "happen to you," which is how many of us live. After the birth of our second child, I wanted to lose my extra pregnancy weight of slightly more than thirty pounds. However, I needed to clearly define my "why" to motivate me toward that goal. In that case, my "why" was to have more energy for my young family, particularly on our upcoming trip to Disney World. So, every morning when the alarm clock woke me at 5:00 a.m. in the dark of early Midwestern winter mornings, I sprang out of bed because I wanted more than anything to be ready for that first Disney trip with my family.

Each of us has the power to choose why we do certain things and how we will move through each day, rather than letting other people, the media, our culture, or situations influence how we make choices and react to our world. For instance, we can be highly annoyed with the train gates that are preventing us from getting to our destination on time—or we can appreciate the extra few minutes in the car to make a quick call to someone we love or to focus our mind on our goals for the week. In the strategic planning of businesses, we formally refer to this as "strategic intent"—the measurable goal toward which we are driving that, once we achieve it, we know we've arrived closer to our desired outcome. Then, we can set a new goal to bring us even further along our dream continuum. So, the aim is to dream boldly and clearly, then focus your resources in the direction of that dream in "chunks" to make it come alive.

American self-help book author and lecturer Dr. Wayne W. Dyer said, "You have a very powerful mind that can make anything happen as long as you keep yourself centered."[8] Keeping ourselves centered and focused on our intent is so important. I could write an entire book about what I've learned about the power of the human mind along my journey. To summarize it quickly for you, your mind has immense potential, and if you can master the ability to utilize its full potential, you will have access to some of the universe's greatest gifts. We have to make a conscious choice to move in the direction we desire. Then, more importantly, we need to support that conscious choice with positive cues for the subconscious mind, which, according to noted researcher Dr. Joseph Murphy (1898–1981), responds to habit and habitual thinking that eventually become beliefs.[9]

We need to habitually paint a picture in our subconscious mind of the dreams we want in our lives so we can train our beliefs to help us give life to those dreams. I do this daily and will explain in later chapters how you can, too.

> *"Do or do not. There is no try."*
> *– Yoda, "Star Wars: The Emperor Strikes Back"*

Action

The final key to Courageous Clarity is action. So far, we've talked about developing congruence in your thoughts and behaviors, removing your adult-acquired mental barriers to dream so you can imagine what you really want in your life, and then vividly painting your innermost desires in your mind so they become a beacon toward which you channel your energy. Well, knowing how to do all of this "head and heart work" is important, foundational work in discovering what we should be putting into our empty place, but until we put it into action, none of it matters. Taking action is what sets apart wildly successful people from those who are not.

To begin, you must discover your inner drill sergeant. I realize this concept may be puritanical to some, but hold on before you judge. I have discovered throughout my life that leading your life (the key word is leading, not following) in a disciplined manner has an untold number of benefits. I'm not suggesting you have no fun. I'm recommending that you actually do the opposite—ensuring you make time for fun and for family, for building relationships, for strengthening your faith, for physical and mental fitness, for work, for self-development, for wealth management, and so on. Unless we take a structured approach to dedicating time for these activities in our lives (including those who matter personally to you), we won't make time for them.

It is clinically proven that the human body thrives on healthy consistency and routine, particularly when it comes to sleeping and waking times.[10] My theory is that this same premise is true for leading one's life and business. When you actively apply the keys to Courageous Clarity consistently, you increase your propensity for truly unlocking all the potential you have within you.

> *"Our life is composed greatly from dreams, from the unconscious, and they must be brought into connection with action. They must be woven together."*
> *— Anais Nin, French-born American*
> *Author of novels and short stories*

I can recall as a new mother having to shift my life to make room for this great new responsibility. My daughter is a terrific blessing, who saved me from the drudgery and detachment of a life on the road four days each week as a management consultant, which is the job I initially interviewed for the fall before I completed my MBA. When my husband and I discovered we were expecting our first child, that plan went out the window; in came the new one to find a way I could contribute my skills and experience to an organization without enduring much travel. When I secured a wonderful position leading marketing for a nonprofit Catholic hospital, I quickly devised a new way to organize my life so I could make time for all of the activities important to me, including the demanding role of motherhood. Now, I will grant you that I was not able to dedicate exactly the amount of time I wished to each task. However, having the ability to do at least a bit of each brought me happiness and the energy I needed to continue growing as a person.

Many of my friends would marvel at my ability to "keep it all together" and remark, "How do you do it?" I would tell them it's no secret. It takes a great deal of positive energy, faith, and self-discipline, as well as a wonderful team—a supportive husband, a nanny, a housekeeper, and family and friends nearby to help when needed. Some women initially think, "God, you had a housekeeper and a nanny? How spoiled!" Or, "What a waste of money!" I do not hide the fact that I had help. But, it clearly was a choice for what kept me happy and fulfilled. Why? Because for women—and for those men who take on the role of house management—keeping a home tidy, babies' laundry washed, bottles clean, toys in order, bedrooms clean, bills paid, home repairs and maintenance in check, and a kitchen fit for meal making is a very hard and time-consuming job. There is no way that a person (man or woman) who works at least 40 hours a week can devote the time it takes to manage a household properly on top of keeping time for family, fitness, faith, relationship building, and self-development. Trying to do so is a sure path to resentment for one's situation in life, not to mention extreme exhaustion.

The Life Balance Myth

My comments here may sound as if I believe work-life balance exists. It may exist somewhere, but I don't want it, that's for sure. Balance suggests that motion is static, that there is no momentum catapulting me forward. I believe the same to be true for many women, particularly those in high-achieving roles. In a New Zealand study of executive women, researchers found that these women CEOs were really making conscious life choices rather than seeking work-life balance.[11] The media in the last several decades has created this notion of mythical work-life balance that, I believe, has set many up for disappointment. Instead of seeking balance, I believe we should seek action toward choices that bring happiness in our lives and success in our businesses.

I would argue that the work-life choices we make aren't really all that segregated or opposed to one another as the phrase would make us believe. As technology improves and allows us to seamlessly flow from one activity to another, we can touch on all of the enriching activities we want to achieve each day one chunk of seconds, minutes, or hours at a time. Business can flow in and out of life and life in and out of business quite effortlessly. They do not need to be two separate entities constantly at battle for your time. The real magic happens when the underlying intentions we carry in our lives reflect those in our businesses. Then, how we spend our time becomes just a series of conscious choices driven by the same set of core values, which I will help you reveal to yourself in the next chapter.

Simply Choosing is Action in Itself

Whatever choice you make, you must choose. You must take action somehow. You must move forward to be of value. Some of my strategic planning and coaching clients may find me very direct and, at times, somewhat demanding. Please know that I do this in the spirit of sparking a change in you and your businesses swiftly. My clients come to me seeking a positive change in their businesses, and that is what I deliver, because I only work with those who are truly seeking clarifying change that leads to more life-giving energy and unlimited potential.

You've already taken your first action toward creating more congruence, aspiration, and intent in your life by reading this book. Now, you must commit to following through on what I lay out in the rest of the book to fully unlock your leadership potential.

CHAPTER 3

CREATING A PATH FOR YOUR
LEADERSHIP POTENTIAL TO FLOW
THROUGH YOUR LIFE AND BUSINESS

Now that you know the four keys to unlock your leadership potential—congruence, aspiration, intent, and action—you must learn how to access them. You can't grow toward your potential through simple awareness of the keys to Courageous Clarity. You need to build a foundation or a path to the keys so they can be used in your life and your business. Throughout the rest of this book, I will ask you to imagine that the keys to Courageous Clarity are a set of four, large, sparkling keys to the locks on a dam behind which is an unlimited source of leadership potential. The challenge is that you are in the dry valley hundreds of feet below the dam, with barren trees around you and so much dust in the air that you can barely see where you are going and the chalky taste in your mouth is suffocating. Through the rest of this book, I will show you how to quickly build an efficient path to those keys. Once you have the keys in hand, you can carefully open the locks of the dam to bring much-needed water to your valley so the dust will settle and your trees of a rich, lush life will grow. To begin building your path, you first will need to embrace your core values.

In my fields of strategic planning and business coaching, we take clients through a core values exercise as one of the first steps in developing a plan. I believe we can apply this same exercise to structures outside of business. In fact, one of my mentors, Loral Langemeier, took me through this exercise several years ago and sparked a wonderful, revolutionary journey toward more clarity in my life. I would like to help you do the same.

> *"These values become an empowering set of personal guidelines that serve as anchor points for leading, coaching, and mentoring others for success. They provide the focus of what people do and why they do it. Values become the convictions that provide the internal stimulus towards a desired or preferred outcome."*
> *— United States Army Field Manual 6-22, Army Leadership*

Once you clarify your core values, which should last your lifetime, making decisions about how you choose to spend your time, your money, your talent, and many other precious resources you have in this life becomes so much simpler. You will begin to build your path toward the keys to Courageous Clarity with the first stepping-stone of identifying your core values. So, let's get down to it.

If you've never studied core values or only touched upon them briefly during a corporate retreat, let's begin with defining core values so we start from the same place. Core values are a set of beliefs and a moral compass that influence the way people and groups behave. They are developed through the totality of your experiences since childhood and reflect the influence of what is handed down to us, such as spiritual traditions, beliefs about life, relationships, and so on. Core values help provide continuity through changes in life and help us make difficult decisions. Many corporations, ministries, and other organizations define their core values during strategic planning exercises. However, it is a rare individual who has defined her core values for her personal life. If only we were taught to define our core values as young adults or even older teenagers, our decisions would be much more well-informed and less "of the moment."

In my experience, core values are those never-changing, fundamental beliefs that you hold so deeply and so firmly in the fabric of your very being that you would not be willing to compromise them for anything—even life itself. This chapter will take you through a series of exercises to help you scratch away at the surface to reveal what is truly important in your life or business. This process should take no longer than 45 minutes. If you've done a similar exercise before or if you have established your core values, I recommend you still complete this exercise to "fit-test" your values to ensure they are true reflections of what lies beneath.

For a list of potential core values, visit www.courageousclaritythebook .com/corevalues to access a list of core values to jump-start your thinking. I update this list as I uncover new terms from my clients that I believe need to be on this list. Certainly the list is not exhaustive, so I encourage you to use your creativity and be true to yourself and/or your business as you develop a list of fifteen potential core values that you hold in high regard or that form the foundation for your enterprise. Pause now to open a browser and download this list while you're thinking about it. Remember, I'm all about action and moving you quickly toward clarity. So, no excuses. Get moving right this moment. If you're driving a vehicle and listening to an audio version of this text, you will need to write a note on a piece of paper at your next safe stop to remember to do this activity when you safely can.

Once you have a list of the top 15 core values that reflect your business and/or your life, you must begin to conduct a "smell test" of these chosen values. What I mean by this is you need to see which ones truly reflect your spirit and/or your business. The way to begin this exercise is to categorize your fifteen core values into those that are highly reflective, those that are moderately reflective, and those that mildly reflect your spirit and/or your business. The trick here is that you are allowed, at most, six values under a category. This forces you to make quick decisions about each value's relative importance. Go ahead and break your list into three categories.

At this point, you should have no more than six values listed in your "highly reflective" category. What I'd like you to do is to take your highly reflective values and place them all on the same level playing field for just one moment. In fact, step away from them, and wherever you are (again, if you're driving a vehicle, you'll need to do this portion later), close your eyes and take 60 seconds to do your best to paint a mental picture on the inside of the front of your skull of the place and time when you have been at your happiest. Just 60 seconds now. When you come back, we'll reveal your true, everlasting core values.

Four, Not Eight, Is Enough

With a fresh, rested, happy, and strong brain and positive outlook, you should now look at the values you scored highly in no order of importance. In fact, letter them A through F (if you have six listed). Ultimately, you are going to create a rank-ordered list (first place, second place, third place, and if necessary, fourth place). You are only going to be allowed to keep up to four of these values. Why no more than four? Clarity requires simplicity. You are going to:

- make some declaratory reminders of these core values;
- state these daily out loud as you begin each day or each business meeting and before making important decisions in either; and
- memorize these values so can recite them to yourself, your life or business coach, and your accountability partner with ease.

Do you see why four is enough? Now, prepare a list with four blank lines on it, and let's get to work.

What I want you to do next is to take value A and ask yourself, "If forced to give up value A for value B, would I do so?" If yes, you know that value B is more important than value A. So, write value B on the top blank line and write value A on the second line. Next, go to value

C and ask yourself, "If forced to do so, would I give up value B for value C?" If no, then proceed to the second line, where value A is. Ask again, "If forced to do so, would I give up value A for value C?" If yes, then you should place value C in second position and move value A to third position. Continue with each value until you have played the trading game with each value against one another. If you're confused, you'll find an example of this exercise at www.courageousclaritythebook. com/tradinggame. It's much easier than it sounds in print. Take several minutes now to complete the trading game to determine your final core value set.

You should have in front of you a rank-ordered list of no more than four core values. At the top is your most important value, the one that supersedes the rest. The second one listed should be one you would be willing to give up to keep number one and so on down the list. Your core value list is unique to you and is not better or worse than others' lists. Our core values are developed through innate thoughts and feelings with which we are born and the influences of the environment (home life, friends, culture, physical space, etc.) around us. What is fascinating, though, is how certain core values are similar across very different cultures.

> *"We must build dikes of courage to hold back the flood of fear."*
> *– Martin Luther King, Jr.*

Contrast, for instance, the cultures of post-Soviet Russia and the United States. Though each country was formed fundamentally under very different circumstances, the people in each nation carry some of the very same core values. I recently met Professor Evgeny Boychencko at a communications conference in Switzerland where he presented research on the values of the Russian people and how they affect the way companies communicate with consumers in that market.[12]

Professor Boychencko stated, "First and foremost, everything in Russia begins with equality." I would argue that this value is quite strong in the United States as well, albeit to a different degree. He went on to explain that the Russian people also value the dream of owning property (which, again, is similar to the American dream). What is interesting, though, is that despite the Russian value for the accumulation of property, Russian people will gladly trade the ability to own property for love of their country and the safety they perceive their government provides them. Professor Boychencko said that Russians know, at any moment, their government can—for the sake of development—use powers similar to those of eminent domain in the United States to take Russians' property. Russians will gladly trade their property dream in the name of fraternity, of standing elbow-to-elbow with their countrymen.[13] Through Professor Boychencko's description of the values in Russian hearts and minds, we can see deep similarities across these very different cultures' core values.

Core Values and Marriage

Knowing our core values not only helps us create more leadership potential in our businesses; it helps us quickly identify others to whom we can relate easily. I'm not a marriage counselor but I'll go out on a limb and say that people who think they've met the person they would like to marry should complete the core values exercise and have their potential spouse do the same. Then, compare and contrast each other's core values, because your values system is one area where opposites usually don't attract. Conflicting values systems can lead to difficulties in money management and parenting, as well as many other marital conflicts. Just one look at the popular dating websites, such as Match.com[14] and eHarmony.com,[15] will show how important they consider core values to be by the emphasis they place on helping you identify your core values in the profile they help you create.

So, if you weren't convinced of the importance of identifying your core values for your business, hopefully the prospect of more rewarding relationships is inspiring enough to motivate you into action today. Place your core values on a paper that you tape to your bathroom mirror, your coffee pot, or anyplace in your home you visit each morning. I also recommend adding them as a screen saver to your computer, your PDA, and other places to remind you of them throughout the day. As you become more familiar with your core values, they will become second nature to you and you can remove these visual cues, if you wish. However, if you live with a supportive accountability partner, I recommend you keep them posted to help that person keep you honest and true to your core values as you begin this awakened phase of your life and/or business. As mentioned earlier, our minds are our most powerful tools, and we must support them to grow. We cannot tap the potential of the subconscious unless we give clear vision to how these core values will manifest themselves into the life we seek.

> *"All you have to do is unite mentally and emotionally with the good you wish to embody, and the creative powers of your subconscious will respond accordingly. Begin now, today, let wonders happen in your life!"*
> *– Dr. Joseph Murphy,* **The Power of Your Subconscious Mind**

Now that you've begun building the path toward the keys to release the power of Courageous Clarity, let's pause for a moment to begin tying everything together for you. Remember your empty place from the first chapter? Do you recall what you listed as activities, emotions, and even people with which you fill your empty place? In looking at the core values you just revealed to yourself, do you see *congruency* between what you value and what you stuff in your empty place? If you don't, this is your first alert that what you are adding to your empty place is working against your pursuit of leadership in your life in some way, shape, or form. For instance, if you regularly hit the snooze button and blow off your morning workout, yet you listed vitality as a core value, you are living inconsistently with your core values. This causes disharmony within. You feel guilty because you're not living the way you want, and your lack of exercise perpetuates your lackluster energy. You create a cycle of disappointment that you may try to remedy with other fillers for your empty place. Subconsciously, you are creating a blurry picture that confuses your inner self. On a business level, the same dissonance occurs when a company values one thing and behaves another way. We must see *congruency*, the first key to Courageous Clarity, between our core values and what we keep in our empty place for us to unlock our full leadership potential.

Keep Your Busy Mind Fixed on Your Heart's Goals

We must carefully and consistently provide our subconscious thoughts a tool that keeps our busy minds fixed on our hearts' goals. The second foundational stepping-stone you need to create on your path toward Courageous Clarity is your dream board, or vision board. This is not a new concept. In fact, you can find out a lot about dream boards on the Internet, complete with explicit instructions. There are even tools like Mind Movies (www.mindmovies.com) that help you bring your dream board "to life" on video. They are a very useful tool that supports our quest for the second key to Courageous Clarity, *aspiration*.

Creating a dream board is quite simple. All you need is a piece of poster board as big as you can fit on a wall you see each morning, plus a stack of old magazines or access to images online that you can print in color. You may get fancier with this exercise if you wish, but I prefer, again, to keep it simple. Clarity thrives on simplicity. As you ponder your life aspirations for the next three to five years, cut out photos, cartoons, graphics, and words that reflect your dreams, and then assemble them in an attractive collage that represents what you would like your life to be like within three to five years. Be bold. Be wild. Be creative, and you will enjoy the end product.

After you complete your dream board, feel free to share it with your accountability partner, your coach, and/or a supportive spouse. If you prefer to keep it private for yourself, that's fine, too. However, you must commit to keeping it where you can see it each morning to remind you of your dreams. If you can, it would be ideal to keep it close to where you spend most of your day so you can absorb its visual cues as many times as possible.

Closing the Loop

Now, it's time for another "close-the-loop moment." Look back at your answers to key Courageous Clarity questions #4, 5, 6, 7, and 9. What currently fills your life, your empty space? What images and audible cues filter through your brain each day? Are they dream board-type images? If not, you need to examine your brain's exposure to outside influences. What you put into your brain daily has a remarkable influence on your ability to unlock your hidden riches. I'll address that in the next chapter.

Surrounding yourself with success images helps train your subconscious mind to guide your intuition on decisions that will get you there. Where a dream board paints a vivid picture of your aspirations, a tool called "I am" statements verbally and audibly commits you to pursuing the endgame in three to five years. In other words, you live daily with the end in mind.

The founder of a fabulous young company SendOutCards, named Kody Bateman, taught me this technique.[16] At a conference in Chicago where I met him, he encouraged me to create a list of statements that I want to be true for myself and those I love in the next three to five years. They should be specific and cover all facets important in your life—relationships, business, spiritual growth, fitness, wealth, and so forth. Examples of "I am" statements are:

- "I am healthy and energetic at my ideal weight of XXX pounds by November 2014."
- "I am celebrating an average annual income of $XXX,XXX by January 2015."
- "I am dedicated to inspiring passion and fulfillment daily in my spouse."

As I said before, I have more than 10 "I am" statements. Though I've memorized most of them, I bring them with me wherever I travel so I may read them aloud to myself at the start of each day to set my frame of mind for the day. Why do I do this? I do this because reading my statements aloud creates positive "self-talk" that teaches my subconscious what I desire to create in my life and the lives of others. The subconscious mind enjoys consistency and repetition. The more my subconscious mind hears my desired "I am" state, the more easily it helps me navigate each day to work toward my leadership potential.

Some of you who read this may think this is all just a bunch of hocus-pocus. However, I assure you it is not. The subconscious mind taps into your intuition, or your hunches or instinct.[17] I've read a wonderful book on the subject by Laura Day, a verified "intuitive," someone who consciously uses intuition in his or her daily or professional life. If you are not yet convinced about your subconscious's power to guide you through your day, I recommend you read her book. To reach your full leadership potential, you must create your "I am" statements, and I am grateful to Kody for introducing me to this concept.

With your "I am" statements, you build a stepping-stone toward *intent,* the third key to Courageous Clarity that unlocks your leadership potential. In your "I am" statements, you need to vividly state your dreams out loud. You are declaring your future and creating it every day. Do you recall your answer to #8 in Courageous Clarity questions? What self-talk do you have now that is positioning you for greatness in your life? You must aspire to a higher standard and live with intent if you are to attain the level of success you seek. With your core values, your dream board, and your "I am" statements, you are building a very clear path to the four keys to Courageous Clarity. You will complete your path to those keys with the final stepping-stone that we'll cover in the next chapter.

CHAPTER 4

§——

COMPLETING YOUR PATH
AND KEEPING IT CLEAR

You are so close to having the four keys to Courageous Clarity in your grasp. I would like to introduce you to the last stepping-stone that completes your path to the keys that unlock your leadership potential. This stepping-stone, more than the others in the last chapter, needs to be polished quite frequently, because doing so will keep you moving forward in *action,* the fourth key to Courageous Clarity.

Action is truly *the* defining key to Courageous Clarity; it separates the best from the rest. Without *action,* all of the other keys to Courageous Clarity are pretty worthless. In their late 1990s work called *The Psychology of Action: Linking Cognition and Motivation to Behavior,* Gollwitzer and Bargh present numerous positive effects of goal-setting in life.[18] While those who are more risk-averse in life might perceive some—or all—action as too risky, another might conclude that there exist just as many dangers lurking in inaction as there are in action, according to money expert Jean Chatsky[19].

If no one has yet introduced you to the value of a short-term tactical plan for your life and your business, I am honored to bring this gem into your consciousness. Loral Langemeier and other master coaches refer to these as "120-day plans," while others use a 180-day format (six months vs. four). Regardless of which duration you choose, the desired outcome of this exercise is to force you to create some realistic and maybe some far-reaching goals to attain; thus, they continue moving you into action. The first step is to clearly state the areas of your life in which you want to gain more leadership/ownership. You must very specific.

A sample of five areas could be:

- Family
- Fitness
- Faith building
- Business
- Financial awareness

This is a very personal tactical exercise, so be precise about what actions you will take in the next time frame (again, 120 or 180 days) to support your growth in your leadership potential. A sample of activities for faith building might be:

TASK	RESOURCES REQUIRED	BY WHEN
Find a spiritual director	Ask friends, seek recommendations from pastor	January 1
Make time for daily meditation before morning workout	Schedule time, both quiet and reflective, in daily calendar	January 15
Attend regular worship services	Schedule time in calendar and companion to attend with	February 1

Of course, not only will your list of areas to improve are unique to your ideas of what leadership means to you, but your list of tasks and the way you approach completing those activities will be different from others' lists.

I've also noticed in working on these with many people that your pacing needs to be compatible with your temperament and desire for speed. I want to trigger you into action, but I don't want your head to spin. That only leads to frustration with your plan. For an electronic template on which to build your plan, visit www.courageousclaritythebook.com/leadershipplan. The template can be customized to your needs and even downloaded to some personal calendar software. My special thanks to health and wealth coach Jim Kaspari of To Your Wealth, LLC, for his work, which served as the basis for Courageous Clarity leadership plan template.

So, create your plan and place an appointment in your calendar to review your progress against your plan each week, or more than once per week if possible. After several weeks, this routine will become your habit. Better yet, grab an accountability partner to help you create your routine and to brainstorm solutions to potential roadblocks to your success. If your accountability partner is not clear on the process you are creating to unlock your leadership power, have an extra copy of this book available for him or her to read. Having an accountability partner is crucial because it is very easy for us to let ourselves "off the hook." Most humans can rationalize their way out of any shortcomings. I've heard many such excuses (including some from myself):

- "I'm just too busy." *Too busy with what? I ask.*
- "My job got in the way." *Why are you choosing your job as your top priority? Is that what you really want?*
- "I'm not sure what to do next." *Then, you need to ask your team for help. Don't have a team, such as a coach or a support group, surrounding your work toward that goal? Then hire a coach, seek a mentor, or join a support group of like-minded people pursuing a related goal.*

Nearly all of us have experienced these same feelings of inadequacy along our journeys, so you are not alone if you find some of these in your consciousness. Now that I've provided you the four stepping-stones (core values, dream boards, "I am statements," and 120-day action plans) you'll need to reach the sparkling keys that unlock the dam behind which lies your leadership potential, you are ready to start your own "revolutionary journey," right?

Yes. And no. If creating more capacity in your life and your business was that simple, you wouldn't see so many life and business coaches vying for your attention. In leadership planning, the "do-it-yourself" method rarely works to its fullest potential. You will need to surround yourself with like-minded people, enriching and sustaining reading material, and in some cases, a good business or life (or both) coach. I highly recommend joining or creating a mastermind group, which is based on the principles of Napoleon Hill, author of the widely read *Think and Grow Rich*, a book that has inspired many to pursue their leadership potential.[20]

"I know the plans I have for you, declares the Lord, plans to prosper you and not to harm you, plans to give you hope and a future." Jeremiah 29:11

In most cases, I find my clients need to "remove some weeds" from their paths to the four sparkling keys. By that I mean, avoid contact with influences that are incongruous and don't support your journey. You may have to limit your contact with friends and associates who don't support your pursuit or are constantly negative and less visionary than you. I also recommend a news "diet." Mainstream media sells fear and sensationalism to attract viewers, and that is exactly what you *don't* need to guide your journey toward your ultimate leadership potential.

What I have provided you are four fundamental elements that open your mind, your heart, and your whole being to the possibilities that await you. In fact, Mark Victor Hansen, another fabulous mentor who is the self-proclaimed "America's Ambassador of Possibility" and mega-selling coauthor of the Chicken Soup for the Soul series of books, has said, "The world is full of possibility. We just need to be open to see it.[21]" You need to reach out to others who encourage your pursuit of what's possible in your life. I can't suggest which groups or types of people for you specifically because that is a matter dependent on your definition of leadership success. For instance, if you want to grow in your development of family relationships, then perhaps a weekend marriage retreat or a parenting course would be appropriate for your growth. Joining a men's club or a women's group might also enrich your journey. If you want to grow your business or potentially start your own business, then you need a business coach, and you need to find a network of other like-minded entrepreneurs. The important part is to not spend so much time researching your support resources that you never seek them. As Mark says, the world is full of possibility. You (and your subconscious mind) just need to be ready to see it all—and I'll add, to quickly take action.

Now that you have all four keys to unlocking your leadership potential

- *Congruency* by defining your core values;
- *Aspiration* by visualizing your desires on a dream board;
- *Intent* by stating out loud, each day, your purpose for your actions; and
- *Action* by forecasting your activities to support your pursuit of life leadership and tracking your progress in a written plan;

you need to know that you must remain vigilant about keeping them front and center in all areas of your life: your relationships, your business, your self-development—everything. Simply knowing Courageous Clarity and applying the four keys to it one time as you read this book will not unlock your full, lifetime leadership potential. Certainly, you'll still possess the keys to the dam, but the stepping-stones upon which you once stood will become slimy, slippery, and indistinguishable from the sticky mud that surrounds them. I suggest you revisit this book and its ideas every twelve months for the first three years after the initial reading so you will more fully internalize these processes.

Once you've successfully applied Courageous Clarity in your life, you'll unlock the dam holding back prosperity, and the stepping-stones will be washed clean by the life-giving water you'll discover behind that dam. With "newly wet ground," your path is bound to become cluttered with weeds and other debris. The events in your life can cause your beautifully polished stepping-stones, which helped you reach your "shiny keys," to become gummed with moss and wet vegetation. These stepping-stones can become covered, making them dangerous and difficult to traverse. If you want to continually grow your leadership power, you need to occasionally weed the path and remove the dead, wet leaves on which you may slip away from your desired outcomes.

As I learned in business school, strategic planning is a process that all companies must repeat as frequently as every 12 months to three years, depending on the industry in which a business operates. Passage of time, changes in the marketplace, and the personal situations of business owner or stockholders are just some of the factors that can shift a company's path. In my consulting practice, we've helped businesses successfully clear their paths so they can continue to thrive and grow. The weeding and application of Courageous Clarity can reveal a slightly shifted, or sometimes an entirely different, path to reach the keys to unlock the dam. Regardless of which season you are in, you must clear your path when the leaves fall and enjoy the beauty of new growth of Courageous Clarity each spring. Applying this same rigorous weeding process to one's life, regardless of what caused the path shift, ensures your continual growth and evolution toward the best version of yourself here on earth. As in the garden and in business, our life paths have a seasonality to them.

Businesses have seven life stages:

- Seed—focus on business planning
- Startup—create market presence and track/manage cash flow

- Growth—establish systems to handle increased volume
- Established—focus on improvement and productivity
- Expansion—add new products/services; expand into new markets
- Decline—search for next venture; cut costs
- Exit—proper valuation and business transition

All businesses go through these seven stages in some shape or fashion. By understanding, appreciating, and applying the four keys to Courageous Clarity (congruency, aspiration, intent, and action) as a business passes through each life stage, owners will unlock the true leadership potential of their enterprises. How, exactly, does a business owner do this?

In my practice, we recommend first digging into the foundation of the business and what is written in the business plan. Examine the core values on which the business was built and how the activity of the business matches up against those core values. If they are not congruent, it is likely the activity needs to change, since the core values typically do not waver through the life stages of a business. Next, review the mission and vision of the business to confirm its aspirations are fully developed and crystal clear. Then, the business, financial, and marketing goals must be fully aligned. To do this, the business may need to make some difficult choices about what it will do versus what it won't do. Its owners must have a clear intention for the endgame of the business: to pass on the organization to the next generation or to exit by going public or being acquired. Finally, to fulfill the goals of the organization, the activity—and those executing the action items—must undergo review. How is a business owner dividing the actions that need to happen to move a business forward? Is she doing most of them herself? Does she have a strong team surrounding her to help with those activities? Are they the proper activities in the first place? Business owners must assess competitors, the marketplace, trends, predicted growth patterns, and more to determine the best activity. In addition, an owner must learn to track that activity to ensure it is leading toward the desired outcome cost-effectively and quickly enough.

Similarly, in life, humans have stages or seasons through which we grow. Reviewing the four keys as we pass through each season (and more frequently as huge shifts happen in our lives) will help maximize our leadership potential. The five stages/seasons in life are:

- Childhood
- Young adult
- Midlife
- Rebirth of youth
- Enlightened

Without realizing it until now, I have applied the four keys in my life as I passed into each season. I intend to continue doing so as I enter each season or encounter a great shift in my thinking or environment. With knowledge, appreciation, and application of these four keys, we can effortlessly find peace with our decisions and happiness in the true sense of knowing we are living as fully as we are intended to do. As we enter each season in life, as in business, we need to reevaluate our use of the four keys to Courageous Clarity because our response to them and our recipes for clarity will evolve as we mature and grow.

Humans begin with the childhood season, when we are in a complete growth phase and play on many different paths chosen for us, sharing the journey with other schoolchildren, children in our neighborhoods, and cousins, while the adults around us carry us along their chosen paths in life. In our young adult season, we research life paths to take, study for them, and work toward acquiring the proper skills and connections to propel ourselves down the paths we choose. By our midlife season, many of us have chosen to pair paths with those of other people and do our best to make our individual paths parallel to—or the same as—our partner's. It is in this midlife season that more than half of those who chose to marry learn that their partners' paths are either not compatible enough with their own or they are not willing to hop off their own path to follow their partners', so they decide to divorce; some remarry in hopes of finding other life partners with paths more harmonious with theirs.

"Lose your dreams and you might lose your mind."
– Mick Jagger

We are seeing the baby boomers redefine what it means to be a "senior" on life's journey. They've turned what used to be the "Golden Years" into the "Rolling Years," right alongside Mick Jagger. They have passed midlife and are experiencing the rebirth of their youth season. Those in the rebirth of their youth season are enjoying the benefits of greater wealth with fewer responsibilities yet the physical ability to still travel, explore, and enjoy life like never before. Most of those I know in the rebirth of their youth season are living very full, happy lives despite the economic delay of their full retirement.

Finally, when we are willing to allow all our years of experience and our mental prowess to overtake the physical self, we enter the enlightened season. This season can be particularly rewarding, as it allows us more time and opportunity to reflect on the prior seasons and how we teach others to live their lives to their fullest potential. Those in the enlightened season should be regarded as having the highest understanding of the four keys to Courageous Clarity because of their years of practicing their application.

CHAPTER 5

GUIDING OTHERS TO DISCOVER
COURAGEOUS CLARITY IN THEIR
LIVES AND BUSINESSES

After you have taken stock of your life in your current season and applied the four keys to Courageous Clarity, your ability to serve others by sharing what you've learned becomes the pinnacle of your experience. The state of clarity is a breeding ground for happiness and can be very contagious. Once you find your clear path in business and in life, you're going to find it difficult to contain your enthusiasm for clarity and the energy it unlocks in your life. You will want others to have that same experience. The side benefit of teaching others to find clarity in their lives is that it locks in what you've learned and refines your vision. Teaching others helps you better internalize a process.

What's beautiful about clarity is that it is available to everyone, regardless of their years in business, age, gender, economic status, religious beliefs, height, weight, golf handicap, shoe size, IQ... anything. It's free, zero calories, and tastes just like you want it to! You just have to desire clarity enough to step outside your normal routine to seek it. That's where we find dissonance that can throw our lives off track.

You see, you are now on the "other side"—the clearer, more energetic side of life. I congratulate you for taking the short time it took to read this book and to learn how to unlock your life's leadership power. Leadership power is about the totality of what this life has to offer— rewarding relationships, business success, spiritual connection with a higher power, vitality, money, and much more. It's about living without regret and about becoming the best version of ourselves while we are here on earth.

Jane's Lesson

As a manager of a customer service call center several years ago, I enjoyed hearing the stories of my employees' weekends with their families. Jane's[22] stories, in particular, were filled with her enthusiasm for seeing her husband very happily fishing at their lake home and sharing boating time with her children and grandchildren. She was very close to retirement and relished the opportunity to visit the lake house so she could prepare large family meals and enjoy at least the limited weekend and vacation time they all had together. Many times, Jane expressed to me how she regretted they didn't spend more time together at the lake house; she dreamed about retirement, when she and her family could do so. Just weeks after my last conversation with Jane, she died shortly after surgery for a heart condition. Jane never got the chance to live her life to the end that she envisioned for herself. She never got the chance to retire. She never got the chance to go back to the lake house to revel in her family's happiness over a large meal. I share her story not to say she did not apply Courageous Clarity. I share Jane's story because many times it has inspired me to live without regret—to not postpone what it is I believe I am meant to do in each season of my life.

To continue your path toward clarity, I encourage you to find an inspiring story—maybe it's your own. To help others unlock their leaders inside, you must first help yourself find power through consistent application of Courageous Clarity. Just like the flight crew says before takeoff: place your oxygen mask on yourself first, then on the child next to you. Follow the keys to Courageous Clarity you've learned. Review your vision board and "I am" statements daily. Know your "why." If your why is not strong enough to make you cry, you need to go deeper and either more truly understand that why or find a new one. In addition, surround yourself with others who live in Courageous Clarity. Doing so will provide you extra fuel to keep Courageous Clarity flowing through your daily decisions and actions. This may require joining a mastermind group of success-minded individuals and may require you spend less time with negative people in your life.

To guide others to discover Courageous Clarity, you must exemplify it boldly and stay true to your convictions. There will be people along your path who will intentionally throw leaves under your feet to make you slip or lose your way, either out of jealousy or misunderstanding. You must hold fast to what it is you truly desire out of your life because no one—not your business partner, nor even your mother or your spouse—is going to want it more for you than you do for yourself. You need to pursue it each day.

Inspiring others to live more clearly begins with an examination of Courageous Clarity outlined in this book. When you hear others complain (which is really the expression of an unspoken need), you may ask them why they don't do something about their complaint. Or, inquire why what they're complaining about is important in their lives. If they can't answer those questions, you can ask whether what they're spending their time on is congruent with their core values (or contributing to the end result they desire, if they have not established core values in their lives). If you find evidence of a lack of congruence, suggest they read this book to help them through their process of finding courage in living their values more clearly.

If they do not wish to read or listen to this book, then they are simply not ready to unlock their own leader inside. You cannot force them. However, that doesn't mean you lack any special training or gifts to influence others. *You have all that you need right inside of you.* God gave each of us all the power we need to succeed right inside of us. Our main responsibility while on this earth is to *firmly believe* this so we can confidently tap into our own inner strength. Then, we need to dig deep to discover our true purpose. Once you discover it, give it all you've got to fulfill your calling!

About the Author,
Denise Stillman, M.B.A.

 Born in the same year that birthed Starbucks, "Willy Wonka and the Chocolate Factory" and Disney World to a German immigrant and second-generation Polish descendant who always wanted more for their children than they had, Denise Stillman used her imaginative mind and tenacity to reach for her goals, exceed them, and bring others success along the way. Denise is a former pharmaceutical marketing consultant and healthcare executive turned energetic entrepreneur, who has founded a successful healthcare business advisory firm in the last three years using *Courageous Clarity*. She developed this philosophy and life-enhancing practice so she could thrive while juggling a busy career and raising two children with her husband, a managing partner at a law firm and beloved little league coach. She is the founder and principal of Clear Directions for Healthcare, a business advisory firm for hospitals and healthcare centers, major medical groups and those who create healthcare products and services. She is a veteran marketer and strategist who has developed expertise in strategic planning, marketing, sales, and business development through her work for well-known consumer products companies, pharmaceutical giants, and the healthcare industry.

With her Clear Directions team, she now brings those skills and talents to bear for leaders in the healthcare industry nationwide.

She has worked with physician leaders for more than 20 years and spent the last half of her career as an employee leading the marketing efforts for a nonprofit community hospital in the Chicago area. Prior to her career in healthcare, she provided counsel to pharmaceutical and consumer products companies including AstraZeneca, Abbott Laboratories, Procter & Gamble, Philip Morris USA, and DowBrands, managing their corporate communications, product marketing, and government relations.

A *summa cum laude* graduate of Bradley University in Peoria, Illinois, Denise holds a bachelor of science degree in public relations, with an emphasis in political science. She also holds an MBA from Northwestern University's Kellogg Graduate School of Management, with emphases in strategy development, marketing, and health services management. She completed a fellowship program in leadership from the Advisory Board Company in Washington, D.C.

She has been recognized for her work by the Public Relations Society of America's Health Academy, the Publicity Club of Chicago, and the *Business Ledger*, which honored her as one of Chicago area's Influential Women in Business 2010. She lives in a Chicago suburb, where she enjoys a very active and fulfilling life with her husband, two children and adoring wheaten terrier.

"We have the power within us for doing good."
—Venerable Mary Potter, LCM
Foundress of the Little Company of Mary Sisters
who will always hold a special place in Denise's heart

"...From everyone who has been given much, much will be required; and to whom they entrusted much, of him they will ask all the more."
Luke 12:48

Doing Good By Giving Back

A portion of the profits from this book will be delivered to the Greater Chicago Food Depository, which distributes 66 million pounds of food, including more than 12.8 million pounds of produce, to 650 pantries, soup kitchens and shelters in Cook County, Ill. Nearly 142,000 men, women and children turn to the Food Depository's network each week, and nearly 678,000 people turn to the network annually.

Contact Information

Denise Stillman is available to speak about how you can unlock your leader within through the power of Courageous Clarity. If you or your company would like to book Denise Stillman for a speaking engagement, contact her office at:

Clear Directions for Healthcare
"Courageous Clarity"
888-316-1761
customerservice@courageousclaritythebook.com

Special pricing on bulk purchases of *Courageous Clarity: Four Keys to Unlock the Leader Inside* is available.

For more information, visit www.courageousclaritythebook.com.

ENDNOTES

1. Rob Kelley, "Most satisfied employees work longer," cnnmoney.com, April 12, 2006. Accessed October 16, 2010. http://money.cnn.com/2006/04/10/pf/bestjobs_survey/index.htm.
2. Names changed to protect privacy.
3. Eileen Blass, "24 million go from 'thriving' to 'struggling'," *USA Today*. Accessed October 16, 2010. http://www.usatoday.com/money/economy/2009-03-09-americandream_N.htm.
4. Mark D. Wolf, "Women-Owned Businesses: America's New Job Creation Engine," *NAWBO Focus*, February 8, 2010.
5. Google. Accessed on February 10, 2010.
6. Matthew Kelly, *Building Better Families: A Practical Guide to Raising Amazing Children* (New York: Ballantine Books, 2008). Audio CD edition.
7. Loral Langemeier, *The Millionaire Maker* (New York: McGraw-Hill, 2006).
8. Dr. Wayne Dyer. Accessed October 16, 2010. http://www.ordinarypeoplecanwin.com/waynedyer.htm.
9. Joseph Murphy, *The Power of Your Subconscious Mind* (New York: Prentice Hall, 1963). Accessed October 16, 2010. http://josephmurphy.wwwhubs.com.
10. National Sleep Foundation. Accessed March 10, 2010. http://www.sleepfoundation.org/sleep-facts-information/myths-and-facts.
11. Judith K. Pringle, University of Auckland; Su Olsson, Massey University; and Robyn Walker, Massey University; Department of Management & Employment Relations, University of Auckland. "Work/Life Balance for Senior Women Executives: Issues of Inclusion?". Paper presented at the CMS 2003 Conference. http://www.mngt.waikato.ac.nz/ejrot/cmsconference/2003/proceedings/gender/Pringle.pdf
12. Professor Evgeny Boychenko. "Individual Consumers' Value Orientation." Presentation at Communications on Top, Davos, Switzerland, February 8–9, 2010.
13. Boychenko, "Individual Consumers' Value Orientation."
14. Match.com is a registered trademark of Match.com, LLC.
15. eHarmony.com is a registered trademark of eHarmony, Inc.
16. SendOutCards is a trademark of SendOutCards, LLC.
17. Laura Day, *Practical Intuition* (New York: Broadway Books, 1997), 10.

18. Peter M. Gollwitzer and John A. Bargh, *The Psychology of Action: Linking Cognition and Motivation to Behavior* (New York: Guilford Press, 1996).
19. Jean Chatsky, The Difference: How Anyone Can Prosper in Even The Toughest Times, (New York: Crown Business, 2009).
20. Napoleon Hill, *Think and Grow Rich* (Meriden, CT: Ralston Society, 1937).
21. Mark Victor Hansen, *Wealthy Writers Wisdom Seminar*. Accessed October 16, 2010. http://www.wealthywriterswisdom.com.
22. Names changed to protect privacy.